HELLO!

THIS IS EARTH!

LAYTON LAVIK

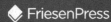 FriesenPress

Suite 300 - 990 Fort St
Victoria, BC, V8V 3K2
Canada

www.friesenpress.com

ISBN
978-1-5255-7344-6 (Hardcover)
978-1-5255-7345-3 (Paperback)
978-1-5255-7346-0 (eBook)

1. JUVENILE NONFICTION, POETRY, HUMOROUS

Distributed to the trade by The Ingram Book Company

HELLO!
THIS IS EARTH!

FOR LINCOLN

Hello. This is Earth!

I've met you before

At the places you go

Both in and out doors.

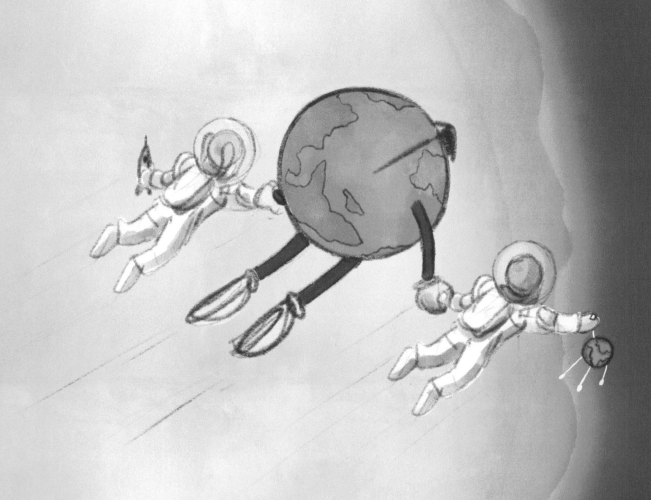

I'm a planet you know

I circle the sun

We call that an orbit

All planets have one.

It takes me one year

To orbit the sun

Come along with me now

We'll have lots of fun.

I'm four and a half
Billion years old
Can you count that high
On your fingers and toes?

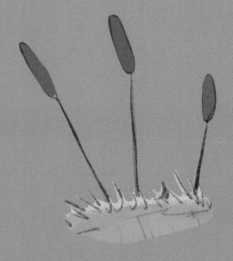

Let's spin round and round

I know the way

For each time I spin

We call that a day.

WINTER

SPRING

SUMMER

FALL

I spin on an axis

That's tilted just so

As I orbit and spin

Seasons come and go.

And look! There's the Moon

Way up in the sky!

It comes out at night

But is always nearby.

The Moon orbits Earth

And is tidally locked.

So we see the same face

On its nightly sky walk.

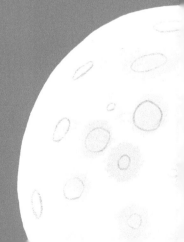

The Sun and the Moon

Both tug on my seas.

This causes the tides,

High and low, in between!

My oceans do cover

Most of my girth

So why do you live

Where it's dry on the Earth?

I have deserts and mountains

Valleys and seas

The snowy white Arctic

Great forests and trees.

Rivers and lakes

Grasslands and bogs

Rain, snow, and sleet

Sunshine and fog.

Way, way down deep

Right down to my core

There's molten rock swirling

Too hot to explore.

My lands they are moving

On tectonic plates

They shift and they shake

And can make the Earth quake!

This moving and shaking

Builds mountains, you know.

Volcanoes erupt

And lava will flow.

Earth is a sphere

I'm shaped like a ball

Like all other planets

One shape fits us all.

Because of my curves

And my orbit and spin

You can watch the Sun rise

And then set at day's end.

Have you ever seen

A magnet so grand?

My magnetic field

Covers all of the land.

From North to South Pole

Reaching out into space

My magnetic force

Helps keep the Earth safe.

My thin atmosphere

Is like a blanket of sky

That helps keep us warm

So life here can thrive.

I'm a unique, rocky planet

As far as we know

There's so much to learn

And places to go.

That pale blue dot

I've been called in the past

You can call me your home

And I'd like it to last.

ABOUT THE AUTHOR

After becoming a father, Layton Lavik wanted to create something special that would allow him to share his passions for science, astronomy and storytelling with his son. As *"Hello! This is Earth"* came to life, he decided to share it with other budding readers in hopes of sparking their curiosity in the universe around us!